What Am I Even Doing Here

Molly Richeson

BookLeaf Publishing

Presentation by *BookLeaf Publishing*

Web: www.bookleafpub.com

E-mail: info@bookleafpub.com

ISBN: 9789357442503

First edition 2023

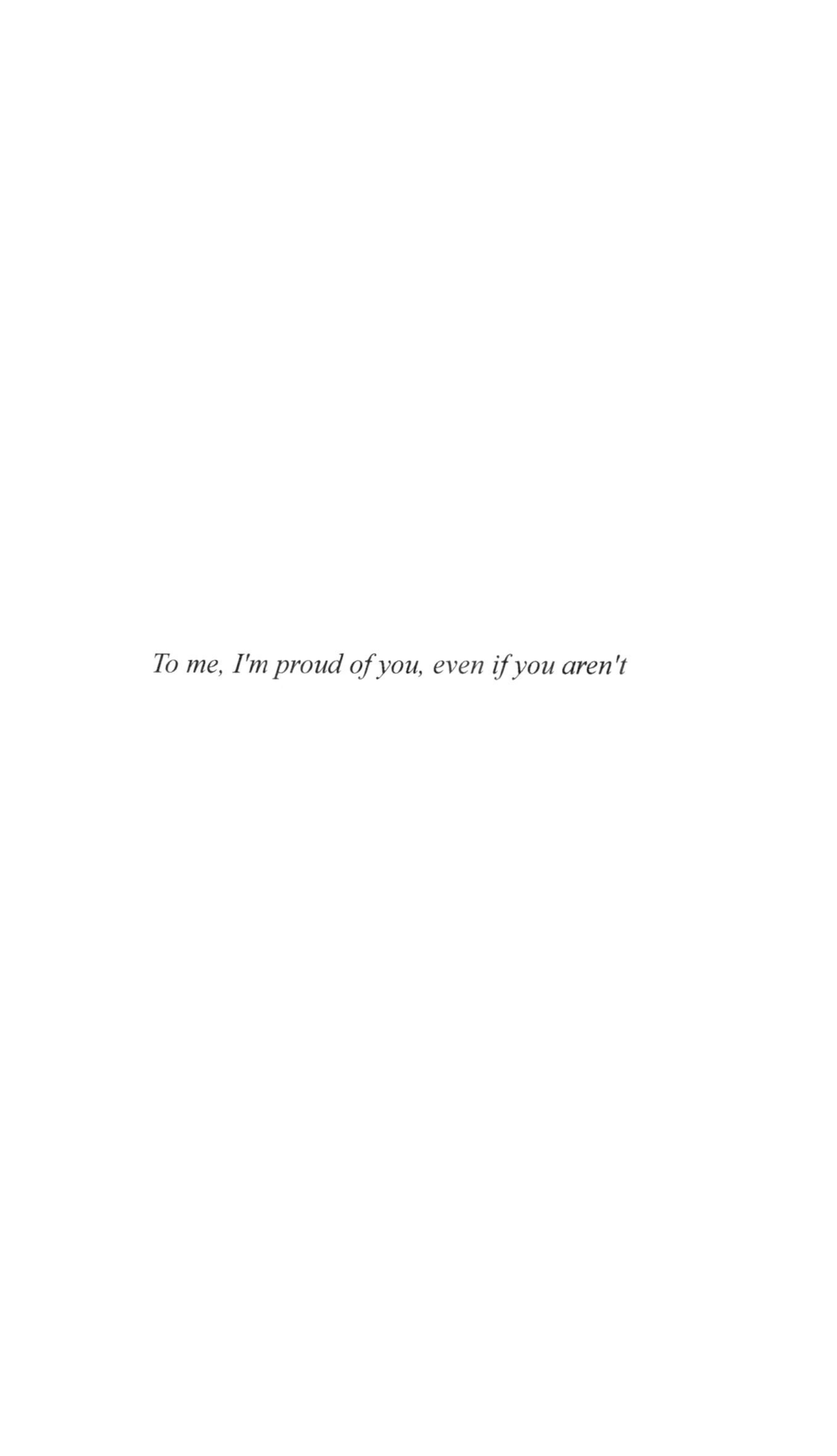

To me, I'm proud of you, even if you aren't

ACKNOWLEDGEMENT

My mother for always having my back
My bestie for being my wifey when I needed
love most
My sisters for lifting my chin when I didn't care
where I was headed
My husband for his patience while we worked
this separation

PREFACE

A small book of bad poems about separation

Just a Heart

I found your picture with my husband's heart
A rule I'm not allowed to break
You're beautiful and "kissing" the camera
My entire soul begins to ache
I asked him; he said you look great
He said he loved to see you shine
I ask him why he's showing love on your things
But refuses to acknowledge mine
He said he's not married to my Facebook
He can do whatever he so please
"I choose Ashley over you" he tells me
And with that, I'm brought to my knees

Wishes

2

I wish you had told me I was beautiful
I wish you had wanted to see me smile
I wish you had felt deep down in your own soul
I'd been left alone now for quite a while
I wish you had just come home to me
I wish you had sat me down to talk
I wish you wouldn't look at me with disgust
I wish you wouldn't rather just walk

Rules

Don't sit next to his brother
He may get the wrong idea
Don't get all dressed up for nothing
We only do that for a reason
Answer the phone promptly
His texts too; don't make him wait
Don't you dare get pregnant with his baby
It's a giant middle finger in his face
Your voice should be soft, sweet, and gentle
Do not "love" pictures of men
Don't talk to those who love yours
Your profile picture should have him
Red hair is meant as a warning
You told him this bit yourself
He chose blonde hair so get it
Take a pill and control yourself
Meet him at the door on arrival
Going out with the girls is a threat
He gets to take credit for our lifestyle
That is not the case with our debt
Stop being such a little white girl
And in arguments you can't use your mind
Don't forget that his job is harder
Don't get between him and his PS5
Twelve entire pages of rules

Efforts to show love and care
I want you to acknowledge the effort
I turn around and there's no one there

Manifest

I wish upon a red candle
I burn frankincense and myrrh
I present my tears to the Goddess
And share my flowers with her
I sing out loud my prayers
I humbly ask for joy
She tells me I'm worth so much more
Than the demands of just some boy
I draw my dreams on mirrors
I write "you're so loved" just the same
She whispers, "Karma's coming,
And she's got my fucking name"
Blessings showered on me
I create it as I speak
Abracadabra and ancestors
It's mine within the week
Time to rest now daughter
Time to smile and dance and sing
Your life will be returned to you
Do not worry for a thing

Silly Heart

My heart is a silly thing
It makes its mind up on its own
Over and over I say, "It's not him"
Over and over it says, "He's the one"

Reminiscing

There are times I look back on us
All the way back in time
I see you walking through the door
I see your eyes briefly meet with mine
I was with someone
You were with someone too
I wonder how much would have changed
If, in that moment, I'd known it was you.

Tava & Travon

I did not carry these babies
I did not give them life
I took on the role of their mother
When I took on the role of his wife
How quickly they stole my heart though
How quickly they shot up and grew
How careful I had to be with them
For us all, this thing was new
I have taken these children as my own
I have nurtured their dreams and their hopes
I have cradled their heads as they cried
I have nearly washed mouths out with soap
Yes, someone did give birth to them
Yes, someone was there before I
And someone cared too little for these two
So I'll love them all the days of my life

Mim

I found a dog at a shelter
She was quiet and kept to herself
She was thin and covered in scars
She had no fur and wet herself
I took this little gremlin with me
I gave her a home and a bath
And a fuckton of antibiotics
I treated the mange on her back
I fed her and cuddled her often
She started to feel more herself
I called her Mad Madame Mim
After a powerful witch like myself
My gremlin is my shadow
My gremlin loves her momma
My gremlin is healthy and happy
And, I, as her person, am honored.

Eli

You were born in the early summer
Your name chosen with so much care
We put so much work into your nursery
And you spent zero time in there!
This big world frightened my darling
He needed his momma holding him tight
I swear to you I was so worried
You'd never sleep through the night
I wanted to be the best for you
I was never quite sure what to do
But regardless of however we started
As time passed, my son, you grew
You've loved trains and heavy machinery
Sharks and science and art
We read all about everything out there
And good god, Eli, you're smart
Right now, you love the military
You want to be a medic someday
You don't know how happy you make me
You don't know how my life you've changed
You're sweet and kind and caring
You're helpful, bright, and fun
I cannot begin to tell you, my darling,
How proud I am to call you "son"

Tucker

Now, it's time for my Tucker
My very last baby, my boy
Oh honey, let Mommy tell you
How you brought her so much joy
You were a big little baby
We struggled together at birth
But sometimes, we fight the hardest
For the things that have the most worth
You bring sunshine into my day
Stars to light up my night
I never know what to expect from you
My little koala who clings to me tight
You are full of laughter
Happiness, tenderness, concern
Sometimes, your little heart gets tender
Sometimes, tears make your eyes burn
No matter, your momma is with you
And you have every piece of my heart
My Oompa Loompa, my Eskimo baby
I've loved you right from the start.

228

We bared our skin
We bared our souls
In that room
We saw each other for what we were
And we loved the hell out of what we saw

Superman

This is my baby
This is my hero
He has my back
It's safe to let my guard down
And just feel the way I actually feel
Without having to hold it back
That's trust
That's love
I was falling and he caught me

Depression

I'm still struggling but I'm not drowning
I'm trying so hard to pull myself together
So I can be the wife he deserves
And the mother all of my children deserve
I don't know why it's so hard for me
After everything, I just feel so raw
And it got to the point that it just hurt
everywhere
All the time
I just want to be able to feel home

GO

15

BEFORE YOU START WRITING
YOU GO FIND THAT MAN
RIGHT NOW
AND LOVE THE HELL OUT OF HIM
STOP EVERYTHING YOU ARE DOING
AND GO TO HIM
IMMEDIATELY
YOU WILL NOT LET HIM LEAVE THIS
HOUSE
WITHOUT KNOWING THAT HE IS
FUCKING PRECIOUS
GO

Boundaries

I love him, but I won't be caged
I'll stand by him but won't take his rage
He has insecurities he needs to overcome
But restricting me more will not be done
I'm won't lead a whisper of a life on tiptoe
I intend to live loudly, bet on that though

The One

I remembered meeting him while I was feeling
sentimental
Looking at him and suddenly, it hit me hard
I knew how I had known he was the one
instinctively
I have missed him since the day I met him.

Remember

18

Remember how you feel right now
Not just the resolve
But the pain and humiliation and exhaustion and
disrespect
You're done
It's over
He needs help and you are not qualified for that
That is not your job
And it is his responsibility
The constant tension and digging
The never-ending stream of shit-talking
You deserve better than that
And your husband is out there waiting for you

Husband

He is patient
He is kind
He does not envy
He does not boast
He is not arrogant or rude
He does not insist on his own way
He is not generally irritable
He is not resentful
He is honest
He takes responsibility
He is respectful of me
He is respectful of my family
He protects me
He trusts me
He hopes
He hopes for us
He fights for us
He never fails me
And our love never fails us

Level Up

It's like standing at the door to the next level of
the game
And it requires the entire team to open
You've spent time getting what you needed to
finish
And even ran around exploring
But you're ready for the next part
Your partner is not
They are running around the field
Chasing chickens for 2 XP each
And any time you suggest moving to the next
level
They get mad and shut their microphone off
Muting you and them both
You have a choice to make at that point:
Stay in this level and continue in this fashion
Until he turns the mic back on
And feels like chickens are getting a little boring
Or go to the next level by disbanding the team
I haven't been waiting minutes by this door
For him to join me
It's been months I've been standing here
Waiting for him to get bored
Talking into the void
Trying to convince him that the rest of the game

Is so much cooler than the chickens
I'm ready to level up
I have leveled up already
And now we just wait
To see if he's going to join me

Here

I'm here at home with my boys
Sleeping in my own bed every night alone
With my wedding ring firmly in place every day
Still keeping things going
And paying for everything
I should be proud
But I view my responsibilities as the most basic
level of effort
And not really anything worth praise
I suppose if I did
I would be proud
I did everything I was supposed to do
I didn't spend a month partying and doing god
knows what
During the three month period I left my family
to fend for themselves
I was here
Being a wife and a mother
I'm good

Hope

I stepped through the door
I evolved
And I can't go back
But I have reached my hand through the door
And he has taken it
I am watching him step through it now
Time for a game plan and a vision
And a whole lotta love